Common Sense for Living: Wise Sayings in Other Words

Dr Beresford Adams

Bee and Gee Publishers, LLC
Bee and Gee International Ministries, Coram, NY
beeandgeepublishers.com

WEB

UPDV

Dedication

Foremost this book is dedicated to my wife and best friend Dr. Gloria Elena Adams. Then, I dedicate this book to the memory my maternal grandmother Emily Bodden Golding whose wit for proverbs was outstanding.

Books by Dr. Beresford Adams

Principles of Belief and Practices of
Faith: A Guide for Successful Living

Make It Plain! A Devotional of Rhema
for Maximizing Your Life

A Psalm to Remember: Belief Matters
and Faith Works

Effective Prayers for Such a Time as
This

beeandgeepublishers.com

Proverbs 25:11

A word fitly spoken is like apples of gold in pictures of silver.

The right word spoken at the right time is as beautiful as gold apples in a silver bowl. **(NCV)**

Like golden apples in silver settings, so is a word spoken at the right time. **(GWD)**

A word properly spoken is like apples of gold in a setting of silver.

Think before you speak. A well expressed thought will last.

A picture is worth a thousand words.

Picture the effects of your words before you give advice.

Words once spoken cannot be taken back so choose them carefully.

To talk without thinking is to shoot without aiming.

Proverbs 26:11

As a dog returneth to his vomit, so a fool returneth to his folly.

Just as a dog returns to his vomit, a fool repeats his folly. **(CJB)**

Like a dog going back to the food which he has not been able to keep down, is the foolish man doing his foolish acts over again. **(BBE)**

Don't keep doing the same thing the same way and expect different results.

If you don't learn from your mistakes you will repeat them.

Don't be a glutton for punishment.

The best job is the job well done the first time.

The fish will soon be caught that nibbles at every bait.

Proverbs 26:15

The slothful hideth his hand in his bosom; it grieveth him to bring it again to his mouth.

A lazy person puts his fork in his food. He wears himself out as he brings it back to his mouth. **(GWD)**

Lazy people may put their hands in the dish, but they are too tired to lift the food to their mouths. **(NCV)**

The lazy person picks up food to eat but is too tired to bring it to his or her mouth.

The art of procrastination is not failing to start something but not completing it.

Don't let procrastination eat your clock.

Genius is 10 percent inspiration, 10 percent preparation, and 80 percent perspiration.

The art of procrastination is being bored by details.

Sudden enthusiasm can result in boredom.

Procrastination is the thief of time.

Proverbs 3:3

Let not mercy and truth forsake thee:
bind them about thy neck;
write them upon the table of thine heart:

Let not loyalty and faithfulness forsake
you; bind them about your neck, write
them on the tablet of your heart. **(RSV)**

Don't ever forget kindness and truth.
Wear them like a necklace. Write them
on your heart as if on a tablet. **(NCV)**

**Remember that you owe everything to
God's mercy and grace.**

**You live each minute through God's
mercy and grace.**

Live each day like it's your last.

Your blessings come from God. Let the hills remind you of that.

Tell the truth and shame the devil.

Some people say, "The church is near but the road icy; the bar is far but I'll drive carefully.

Speak the truth but leave immediately.

Sometimes I go about pitying myself, and all the time I am being carried by God.

Truth and oil always come to the surface.

Proverbs 3:5

*Trust in the LORD with all thine heart;
and lean not unto thine own
understanding.*

*Trust the LORD with all your heart,
and don't depend on your own
understanding.* **(NCV)**

*Trust in the LORD with all your heart,
and do not rely
on your own insight.* **(RSV)**

Leave the driving to God.

**God is your lawyer in the court room,
your doctor in the sick room, and your
all in all.**

Trust in God, but mind your own business.

Don't stay up at nights worrying about your problems. Remember God doesn't sleep and doesn't need your company.

Don't worry; God has a plan.

Proverbs 3:6

*In all thy ways acknowledge him,
and he shall direct thy paths.*

*Remember the LORD in all you do, and
he will give you success.* **(NCV)**

*In all your ways acknowledge Him, And
He shall direct your paths.* **(NKJV)**

Put God first and you won't be last.

**Wherever you are going God is
already there and wherever you came
from God is still there.**

Proverbs 4:26

*Ponder the path of thy feet,
and let all thy ways be established.*

*Be careful what you do, and always do
what is right.* **(NCV)**

*Level the path for your feet, let all your
ways be properly prepared.* **(CJB)**

Don't be your worst enemy.

Look before you leap.

**If you make your bed hard you might
have to sleep on it.**

If you spit in the wind it might hit you
in your face.

Don't set traps for others you might
get caught in them.

In baiting a mousetrap with cheese,
always leave room for the mouse.

Proverbs 9:10

*The fear of the LORD is the beginning of
wisdom:
and the knowledge of the holy is
understanding.*

*Wisdom begins with respect for the
LORD, and understanding begins with
knowing the Holy One. **(NCV)***

*The fear of the LORD is the beginning of
wisdom, and the knowledge of the Holy
One is insight. **(RSV)***

**Who can counsel God and who is wiser
than God?**

**No one knows anything except what
God wants us to know.**

If you fear God, you won't fear humans.

You can't get up early enough to fool God.

Fear not the person who fears God.

Proverbs 10:12

Hatred stirreth up strifes:but love covereth all sins.

Hatred stirs up trouble, but love forgives all wrongs. (NCV)

Hate starts quarrels, but love covers every wrong. (GWD)

Always consider the source of an argument it might be more about dislike than reality.

Whatever is written on the forehead is always seen.

Love is the antidote to the poison of hate.

What one knows it is sometimes useful
to forget.

Do not wrong or hate your neighbor
for it is not that person who you wrong
or hate but yourself.

The one who loves does not hate.

Those who love you will make you
weep; those who hate you will make
you laugh.

Don't try to make someone hate the
person he or she loves, for he or she
will still go on loving, but they will hate
you.

In order to really love someone you
must love him or her as though they
were going to die tomorrow.

Proverbs 11:13

*A talebearer revealeth secrets:
but he that is of a faithful spirit
concealeth the matter.*

*Gossips can't keep secrets, but a
trustworthy person can.* **(NCV)**

*One who brings gossip betrays a
confidence, But one who is of a
trustworthy spirit is one who keeps a
secret.* **(HNV)**

**A gossiper cannot be trusted but a
faithful person shows integrity.**

Remember when you tell secrets to your best friend that your best friend has a best friend.

There is gossip every day, but if no one listens the gossip will die.

A dog who brings a bone takes a bone.

To whom you tell secrets, to them you resign your liberty.

Ask a gossiper: "Do I need to know this?"

A finger that points to others can point to you also.

The person who comes to you with a story takes two away from you.

The person who does not know one thing knows another.

A spoken word is like a sparrow that once has flown away, cannot be caught again.

It is not a secret if it is known by three people.

Nothing is as burdensome as a secret.

Gossipers are the devil's trumpeters.

Wolves never gossip about each other.

A gossiper's mouth is the devil's mailbag.

A rumor goes in one ear and out many mouths.

Silence is golden.

A silent mouth is melodious.

A lie travels around the world while truth is putting its boots on.

A closed mouth catches no flies.

Two dogs fight for a bone, and a third runs away with it.

Slander slays three persons: The speaker, the spoken to, and the spoken of.

No sooner have you spoken than what you have said becomes the property of another.

It is easier to dam a river than to stop a gossip.

A gossip needs no carriage.

Gossiping and lying go hand in hand.

Gossipers always suspect that others are talking about them.

Proverbs 11:24

There is that scattereth, and yet increaseth;
and there is that withholdeth more than is meet,
but it tendeth to poverty.

Some people give much but get back even more. Others don't give what they should and end up poor. **(NCV)**

Some give freely and still get richer, while others are stingy but grow still poorer. **(CJB)**

Feely give, freely receive.

An open hand that gives also receives.
Give graciously, even an onion.

God gives nothing to those who keep
their arms crossed.

God gives, but he doesn't sell.

Alms given openly will be rewarded in
secret.

Forget the favors you have given;
remember those received.

Gifts reflect those who give them.

The scent of a rose will always stay on
the hand of the giver.

The more you sow is the more you
grow and the more you grow is the
more you reap.

There is no better sale than when you
give a true friend what he or she needs.

What you give you get, ten times over.

God gives but does not lock the gate.

More grow in the garden than the
gardener knows he or she has sown.

Proverbs 12:11

*He that tilleth his land shall be satisfied
with bread:
but he that followeth vain persons is void
of understanding.*

*Those who work their land will have
plenty of food, but the one who chases
empty dreams is not wise.* **(NCV)**

*Whoever works his land will have plenty
to eat, but the one who chases unrealistic
dreams has no sense.* **(GWD)**

Don't expect to eat if you don't work.

**The teeth chew that the stomach may
rejoice.**

Work is the medicine for poverty.

The way one eats is the way one works.

Work relieves us from three great:
Evils, boredom, vice, and want.

Pray as though no work could help,
and work as though no prayer could
help.

Work is our business; its success is
God's.

You don't satisfy your hunger by
watching others work.

Don't try to buy diamonds with the
money that you have to buy ice.

Proverbs 12:15

*The way of a fool is right in his own eyes:
but he that hearkeneth unto counsel is wise.*

Fools think they are doing right, but the wise listen to advice. **(NCV)**

The way of a fool is right in his own eyes, but a wise man listens to advice. **(RSV)**

It is foolish to always take your own advice.

A health care professional who treats his or herself might have a fool for a patient.

The baker's children never have
bread.

A spoon does not know the taste of
soup, nor a learned fool the taste of
wisdom.

It is the barber who always needs a
haircut.

The person who asks is a fool for five
minutes, but the person who does not
ask remains a fool forever.

The only stupid question is the one
that is not asked.

A wise person never knows all, only
fools know everything.

Only a fool tests the depth of the water with both feet.

A wise person learns at the fool's expense.

Proverbs 12:16

*A fool's wrath is presently known:
but a prudent man covereth shame.*

*Fools quickly show that they are upset,
but the wise ignore insults.* **(NCV)**

*A fool's anger is known at once, but a
cautious person slighted conceals his
feelings.* **(CJB)**

**Sometimes it's better to grin and bear
it.**

Don't let them see you sweat.

**Take thy thoughts to bed with thee, for
the morning is wiser than the evening.**

A fool in a hurry drinks tea with a fork.

A nail that sticks up will be hammered down.

Anger can be an expensive luxury.

Anger without power is folly.

Proverbs 25:14

Whoso boasteth himself of a false gift is like clouds and wind without rain.

People who brag about gifts they never give are like clouds and wind that give no rain. **(NCV)**

As clouds and wind without rain, so is one who takes credit for an offering he has not given. **(BBE)**

Promises have legs. Only a gift has hands.

Hot air rises.

If it sounds hallow it is probably empty.

The devil always takes back his gifts.

What is bought is cheaper than a gift.

Take gifts with a sigh; most people
give to be paid.

A loan, though old, is not a gift.

Proverbs 27:5

Open rebuke is better than secret love.

It is better to correct someone openly than to have love and not show it. **(NCV)**

Open criticism is better than unexpressed love. **(GWD)**

Sometimes it is better to correct a person frankly than to not to do so out of love.

Be plainspoken with others when necessary and do not fear that you might hurt their feelings.

Don't spare a person's feeling only to devastate them later.

Better to use a swatter on a person's forehead to kill a fly than to use a hatchet later.

Proverbs 14:9

Fools make a mock at sin: but among the righteous there is favour.

Fools don't care if they sin, but honest people work at being right. **(NCV)**

Stubborn fools make fun of guilt, but there is forgiveness among decent people. **(GWD)**

You reap what you sow.

Forgiveness is the fragrance the violet sheds on foot that crushed it.

Proverbs 23:1

*When thou sittest to eat with a ruler,
consider diligently what is before thee.*

*If you sit down to eat with a ruler, notice
the food that is in front of you.* **(NCV)**

*When you sit down to dine with a ruler,
think carefully about who is
before you.* **CJB)**

There is no free lunch.

**You won't get everything you pay for
but everything you get you will pay
for.**

Watch out for the fox that seems like it's guarding the hen house.

The only free cheese is in the mouse trap.

Always count the cost of a favor.

It's not who you know but who knows you.

With foxes we must play the fox.

Proverbs 14:10

The heart knoweth his own bitterness; and a stranger doth not intermeddle with his joy.

No one else can know your sadness, and strangers cannot share your joy. **(NCV)**

The heart knows its own bitterness, and no stranger shares its joy. **(RSV)**

In sorrow the half is often not told.

You don't know what the Lord has done for me.

Sadness is a valuable treasure, only discovered in people you love.

Joy and sorrow sleep in the same bed.

The bridge between joy and sorrow is
not long.

The right hand doesn't always know
what the left hand is doing.

Proverbs 14:12

There is a way which seemeth right unto a man, but the end thereof are the ways of death.

There is a way that seems right to a person,
but eventually it ends in death. **(GWD)**

Some people think they are doing right,
but in the end it leads to death. **(NCV)**

All that glitters is not gold.

The right way is God's way.

It is easy to frighten the bull from the window.

What is wrong today won't be right tomorrow.

Proverbs 25:15

*By long forbearing is a prince
persuaded, and a soft tongue breaketh
the bone.*

*With patience you can convince a ruler,
and a gentle word can get through to the
hard-headed.* **(NCV)**

*With patience a ruler may be persuaded,
and a soft tongue
will break a bone.* **(RSV)**

**You catch more flies with honey than
vinegar.**

**If you throw a sponge against a wall it
won't break.**

Patience is bitter but its fruit is sweet.

Have patience, the grass will be milk soon enough.

Patience is a virtue.

Patience is poultice for all wounds.

A moment of patience can prevent a great disaster and a moment of impatience can ruin a whole life.

One minute of patience can mean ten years of peace.

Patience is the most beautiful prayer.

The salt of patience seasons everything.

Patience begins with tears and ends with a smile.

Proverbs 22:13

The slothful man saith, There is a lion without, I shall be slain in the streets.

A lazy man says,
"There's a lion outside! I'll be killed if I go out in the street!" **(CJB)**

The hater of work says, There is a lion outside: I will be put to death in the streets. **(BBE)**

It is always easy to find an excuse.

There is difference between an excuse and a reason.

The person who can't dance says the band can't play.

A bad worker blames the tools.

Only losers say "Winning isn't everything."

Blame is a lazy person's wages.

Excuses are always mixed with lies.

Where there is a will there is a way. Where there is no will there is an excuse.

Every error has its excuse.

A lazy messenger is not short of excuses.

Proverbs 14:13

Even in laughter the heart is sorrowful;
and the end of that mirth is heaviness.

Someone who is laughing
may be sad inside,
and joy may end in sadness. **(NCV)**

Even while laughing a heart can ache,
and joy can end in grief. **(GWD)**

Sometimes laughter is just crying on the inside.

People often laugh to cover up hurt feelings.

Laughter is not good medicine if you don't deal with the hurt inside of you.

The person who flatters you with laughter wants to see you cry.

Proverbs 25:19

Confidence in an unfaithful man in time of trouble is like a broken tooth, and a foot out of joint.

Trusting unfaithful people when you are in trouble is like eating with a broken tooth or walking with a crippled foot. **(NCV)**

Relying on an untrustworthy person in a time of trouble is like relying on a broken tooth or an unsteady leg. **(CJB)**

When in trouble don't rely on those who hurt you when things were going well with you.

Using a weak cane for a walking stick can do you more harm than good.

Even a dog can distinguish between being stumbled over and being kicked.

Don't pour water into barrels with holes.

The hole is more honorable than the patch.

Proverbs 16:3

*Commit thy works unto the LORD,
and thy thoughts shall be established.*

*Entrust your efforts to the LORD, and
your plans will succeed.* **(GWD)**

*Depend on the LORD in whatever you
do, and your plans will succeed.* **(NCV)**

**It is God who helps the person with
one arm to beat grains.**

**You can plant and water but it is God
who gives the increase.**

Proverbs 16:18

*Pride goeth before destruction,
and an haughty spirit before a fall.*

*Pride goes before destruction, and
arrogance before failure.* **(CJB)**

*Pride precedes a disaster, and an
arrogant attitude precedes a fall.* **(GWD)**

**Don't try to catch the ball before it
reaches you.**

**People appoint but God can
disappoint.**

**You cannot do anything unless God
gives you the strength.**

Don't throw your hat so high that you can't reach it.

Failure is not falling down; you fail when you don't get back up.

Don't watch where you fall, watch where you slip.

Pride is the mask of one's own faults.

Meekness is the pride of the humble.

Too much humility is pride.

Proverbs 22:6

Train up a child in the way he should go: and when he is old, he will not depart from it.

If a child is trained up in the right way, even when he is old he will not be turned away from it. **(BBE)**

Train children how to live right, and when they are old, they will not change. **(NCV)**

A stitch in time saves nine.

Why close the barn after the horse has left?

Children should be taught not bought.

There is nothing sadder than an adult stuck in childhood.

When a twig grows hard it is difficult to twist it. Every beginning is weak.

Proverbs 26:1

As snow in summer, and as rain in harvest, So honor is not seemly for a fool.

It shouldn't snow in summer or rain at harvest. Neither should a foolish person ever be honored. **(NCV)**

Like snow in summer or rain at harvest-time, so honor for a fool is out of place. **(CJB)**

Undeserved success doesn't last and misplaced honor can be destructive.

Rewarding incompetence is like giving a person a backpack for a parachute.

The person who wants to sell his or her honor will always find a buyer.

Where there is no shame, there is no honor.

Undeserved praise is mockery disguised.

Proverbs 26:4

Answer not a fool according to his folly, Lest thou also be like unto him.

Don't give fools a foolish answer, or you will be just like them. **(NCV)**

Do not answer a fool with his own stupidity, or you will be like him. **(GWD)**

Don't be a part of unhealthy conversations they might become about you.

Never is a man in more need of his intelligence than when a fool asks him a question.

Familiarity with some people can be a form of contempt.

Where ignorance is bliss 'tis folly to be wise.

Birds of the same feather flock together.

The right answer to a fool is silence.

Show me your company and I will tell you who you are.

If you lie down with dogs you will get up with fleas.

When one dog barks others will join it.

Live with wolves and you learn to howl.

Pick your friends like you pick your fruits.

Proverbs 15:1

*A soft answer turneth away wrath:
but grievous words stir up anger.*

*A gentle answer will calm a person's
anger, but an unkind answer will cause
more anger.* **(NCV)**

*A gentle response deflects fury, but a
harsh word makes tempers rise.* **(CJB)**

**Don't throw fuel on a fire and expect it
to go out.**

It takes two to tango.

Use soft words and hard arguments.

Anger is a stone cast into a wasp's nest.

Anger is always more harmful than the insult that caused it.

The best answer to anger is silence.

Proverbs 16:2

All the ways of a man are clean in his own eyes;
but the LORD weigheth the spirits.

You may believe you are doing right, but the LORD
will judge your reasons. **(NCV)**

A person thinks all his ways are pure, but the LORD weighs motives. **(GWD)**

God sits high and looks low.

You may fool some people sometimes, most of the people most of times, or even think that you can fool

all the people all the times, but you can't fool God any of the times.

Take away the motive, and the sin is taken away.

One does not give without a motive.

Proverbs 22:1

A good name is rather to be chosen than great riches, and loving favour rather than silver and gold.

A good name is more to be desired than great wealth, and to be respected is better than silver and gold. **(BBE)**

Being respected is more important than having great riches. To be well thought of is better than silver or gold. **(NCV)**

We live our eulogies and we write our epitaphs.

Let your good works speak for you.

Life is for one generation; a good name is forever.

A good name is a second inheritance.

He who leaves a good name does not die poor.

A good name is better than a good face.

A good reputation should not just precede you it should follow you.

A person is judged by his or her deeds, not by his or her words.

Words without deeds are like a garden full of weeds.

A person that breaks his or her word
is like asking others to lie for them.

The work praises the person.

Proverbs 26:14

As the door turneth upon its hinges,
So doth the sluggard upon his bed.

As a door turns on its hinges, So does the
lazy man on his bed. **(NKJV)**

Like a door turning back and forth on its
hinges, the lazy person turns over and
over in bed. **(NCV)**

There are lazy people who are busy
going no place.

There is a difference between busy and
producing and busy and being
unproductive.

A lazy person and a warm bed are difficult to part.

Lazy people get active when it's time to sleep.

Proverbs 27:17

Iron sharpeneth iron; So a man sharpeneth the countenance of his friend.

As iron sharpens iron, so people can improve each other. **(NCV)**

Just as iron sharpens iron, a person sharpens the character of his friend. **(CJB)**

Opposition and competition can make you a better person.

"Yes" people don't make you a better person.

Proverbs 27:21

The refining pot is for silver, and the furnace for gold; And a man is tried by his praise.

A hot furnace tests silver and gold, and people are tested by the praise they receive. **(NCV)**

The crucible tests silver, and the furnace tests gold, but a person is tested by his reaction to praise. **(CJB)**

A person's character can be measured by how much his or her head swells when they are honored.

Don't seek a crown without a cross.

If you want to judge people's characters, give them power.

Some people want to be praised for the rest of their lives for what they have done well for one day.

Don't praise the bread that is not out of the oven.

Praise the ripe field, not the green corn.

Pay the doctor, praise the Lord.

Abuse often starts with praise.

Proverbs 26:5

Answer a fool according to his folly,
Lest he be wise in his own conceit.

Answer a fool with his own stupidity, or
he will think he is wise. **(GWD)**

But answer fools as they should be
answered, or they will think they are
really wise. **(NCV)**

You can act dumb and still be wise.

Don't throw your pearls to animals as
food.

A fool is like other people as long as he
or she remains silent.

Proverbs 22:3

*A prudent man foreseeth the evil,
and hideth himself: but the simple pass
on, and are punished.*

*The sharp man sees the evil and takes
cover: the simple go straight on and get
into trouble.* **(BBE)**

*Sensible people foresee trouble and hide
from it, but gullible people go ahead and
suffer the consequence.* **(GWD)**

You can't duck what you don't see.

**The fool does what he can't avoid; the
wise person avoids what he or she
can't do.**

Where there is smoke assume that there is fire.

Clouds gather before a storm.

Wise people ask questions of themselves; the fool questions others.

The person who foresees affairs three days in advance would be rich for a thousand years.

When the mouse laughs at the cat, there is a hole nearby.

A prudent person does not make the goat his gardener.

To know the road ahead ask those returning.

To see the valley, go up to the mountain.

If you want to die young make your physician your heir.

Proverbs 27:1

Boast not thyself of tomorrow; For thou knowest not what a day may bring forth.

Don't brag about tomorrow; you don't know what may happen then. **(NCV)**

Do not brag about tomorrow, because you do not know what another day may bring. **(GWD)**

Don't count your chickens before they hatch.

Blue skies don't mean it won't rain soon.

No one knows what tomorrow will bring.

Tomorrow the sun may not rise.

Never put off till tomorrow what may be done today.

One of these days is none of these days.

Yesterday is but a dream, tomorrow is but a vision. But today well lived makes yesterday a dream of happiness, and every tomorrow a vision of hope. Live well, therefore, this day.

When you were born, you cried and the world rejoiced. Live your life each day that when you die, the world cries and you rejoice.

Today is the first day of the rest of
your life.

No time like the present.

Don't count the days, make the days
count.

Tomorrow never comes.

Talk about things of tomorrow and the
mice in the ceiling laugh.

Don't cross a bridge before you come
to it.

Proverbs 26:20

For lack of wood the fire goeth out;
And where there is no whisperer,
contention ceaseth.

If there's no wood, the fire goes out; if
nobody gossips, contention stops. **(CJB)**

Without wood, a fire will go out,
and without gossip,
quarreling will stop. **(NCV)**

Gossips fuel arguments.

Trash talk causes fire.

It takes two to argue and a gossip to keep it going.

The quarrel of the sheep doesn't concern the goats.

They quarrel about an egg and let the hen fly.

When shepherds quarrel, the wolf has a winning game.

Proverbs 27:2

*Let another man praise thee,
and not thine own mouth; a stranger,
and not thine own lips.*

*Praise should come from another person
and not from your own mouth,
from a stranger and not from your own
lips.* **(GWD)**

*Let another man praise you, and not your
own mouth; A stranger, and not your
own lips.* **(UPDV)**

Self praise is no recommendation.

**Nice people may finish last but Jesus
said: "The first shall be last."**

People blame themselves for the purpose of being praised.

The lizard that jumped from the high iroko tree to the ground said he would praise himself if no one else did.

Proverbs 27:3

*A stone is heavy, and the sand weighty;
but a fool's wrath is heavier
than them both.*

*A stone is heavy, And sand is a burden;
But a fool's provocation is heavier than
both.* **(HNV)**

*Stone is heavy, and sand is weighty,
but a complaining fool is worse than
either.* **(NCV)**

Too much complaining is depressing.

**A depressed person can weigh you
down with his or her constant
complaints.**

Better to meet a bear robbed of her cubs than a person in his or her folly.

A person who was always complaining was quite rightly sent to hell. "Why are you burning damp wood?" was the person's first comment.

The lazy person sweats when they eat and complain of the cold when they work.

Proverbs 27:4

*Wrath is cruel, and anger is outrageous;
but who is able to stand before envy?*

*Anger is cruel
and destroys like a flood, but no one can
put up with jealousy!* **(NCV)**

*Wrath is cruel, and angry feeling an
overflowing stream; but who does not
give way before envy?* **(BBE)**

Anger makes some people cruel.

Anger is a child of envy.

It is easier to control anger than envy.

Proverbs 27:6

Faithful are the wounds of a friend;
but the kisses of an enemy are deceitful.

The slap of a friend can be trusted to
help you, but the kisses of an enemy are
nothing but lies. **(NCV)**

Faithful are the wounds of a friend;
Although the kisses of an enemy are
profuse. **(WEB)**

Flattery is not always the best form of a compliment.

A friend will confront you while an enemy will mock you.

A faithful friend is medicine for life.

Flattery makes friends and truth makes enemies.

Both your friend and your enemy think you will never die.

Stars are not seen by sunshine.

Take heed of enemies reconciled, and meat twice boiled.

When there is no enemy within, the enemies outside can't hurt you.

An enemy will agree but a friend will argue.

Keep your friends close but your enemies closer.

Proverbs 27:7

*The full soul loatheth an honeycomb;
but to the hungry soul every bitter thing
is sweet.*

*One who is full despises honey, but to
one who is hungry, even bitter food tastes
sweet.* **(GWD)**

*When you are full, not even honey tastes
good, but when you are hungry, even
something bitter tastes sweet.* **(NCV)**

**You won't miss the well until it runs
dry.**

**An empty stomach doesn't remember
the last time it was full.**

Proverbs 27:8

As a bird that wandereth from her nest, so is a man that wandereth from his place.

Like a bird that wanders from her nest, So is a man who wanders from his home. **(NASB)**

Like a bird that strays from its nest is a man who strays from his home. **(CJB)**

Know which side of your bread is buttered.

There is no place like home.

The child who loves freedom is the first victim of it.

Proverbs 27:9

*Ointment and perfume rejoice the heart:
so doth the sweetness of a man's friend
by hearty counsel.*

*Oil and perfume make the heart glad,
So a man's counsel is sweet
to his friend.* **(NASB)**

*The sweet smell of perfume and oils is
pleasant, and so is good advice from a
friend.* **(NCV)**

A friend in need is a friend indeed.

No person is an island.

God provides what you need and it is always closer than you think.

Good advice is often annoying, bad advice never.

Proverbs 27:10

Thine own friend, and thy father's friend, forsake not; neither go into thy brother's house in the day of thy calamity: for better is a neighbour that is near than a brother far off.

Do not forsake your own friend or your father's friend, And do not go to your brother's house in the day of your calamity; Better is a neighbor who is near than a brother far away. **(NASB)**

Don't forget your friend or your parent's friend. Don't always go to your family for help when trouble comes.
A neighbor close by is better than a family far away. **(NCV)**

Drop your bucket at the nearest well.

A bird in the hand is better than two in the bush.

The road to a friend's house is never long.

Proverbs 27:11

My son, be wise, and make my heart glad, that I may answer him that reproacheth me.

Be wise, my son, and make my heart glad so that I can answer anyone who criticizes me. **(GWD)**

Be wise, my child, and make me happy. Then I can respond to any insult. **(NCV)**

Always seek to have a peaceful home that you can deal with this tumultuous world.

The tongue and teeth will meet but they should serve the same purpose.

A person makes his or her home where the living is best.

Proverbs 3:32

For the froward is abomination to the Lord: but his secret is with the righteous.

The LORD hates those who do wrong, but he is a friend to those who are honest. **(NCV)**

The devious person is disgusting to the LORD. The LORD's intimate advice is with decent people. **(GWD)**

The Lord seeks those who are close to God's heart.

What you do in the dark will be revealed in the light.

Try praying. Nothing pleases God more than to hear a strange voice.

Proverbs 3:26

*For the LORD shall be thy confidence,
and shall keep thy foot from being taken.*

*Because the LORD will keep you safe.
He will keep you
from being trapped.* **(NCV)**

*The LORD will be your confidence. He
will keep your foot
from getting caught.* **(GWD)**

**God prefers a straightforward person
over a person who has his own her
agendas.**

**God knows where all the traps in your
life are.**

Proverbs 13:12

Hope deferred maketh the heart sick: but when the desire cometh, it is a tree of life.

It is sad not to get what you hoped for. But wishes that come true are like eating fruit from the tree of life. **(NCV)**

Hope deferred makes the heart sick, but a desire fulfilled is a tree of life. **(RSV)**

Delayed hope may make you sick but when it finally comes you are made glad.

You have to kiss a lot of toads before you find a handsome prince.

While there's life there's hope.

The smaller the lizard is the greater the hope of becoming a crocodile.

Proverbs 15:13

A merry heart maketh a cheerful countenance: but by sorrow of the heart the spirit is broken.

A joyful heart makes a cheerful face, But when the heart is sad, the spirit is broken. **(NASB)**

A glad heart makes a face happy, but heartache breaks the spirit. **(CJB)**

Often what you see is what you get.

When we sing everybody hears us, when we sigh nobody hears us.

Even in laughter the heart may ache,
and joy may end in grief.

You can never be happy at the expense
of the happiness of others.

Proverbs 10:4

He becometh poor that dealeth with a slack hand:but the hand of the diligent maketh rich.

A lazy person will end up poor, but a hard worker will become rich. **(NCV)**

He who is slow in his work becomes poor, but the hand of the ready worker gets in wealth. **(BBE)**

Hard work pays off.

The early bird gets the worm.

God helps those who help themselves.

God is a busy worker but loves to be helped.

Call on God, but row away from the rocks.

God gives the nuts but God doesn't break them.

Roasted pigeons will not fly into one's mouth.

God gives birds their food but do not drop it in their nests.

Proverbs 10:2

Treasures gained by wickedness do not profit, but righteousness delivers from death.

Wealth which comes from sin is of no profit, but righteousness gives salvation from death. **(BBE)**

Riches gotten by doing wrong have no value, but right living will save you from death. **(NCV)**

What if you gain the whole world and lose your soul?

The jay bird doesn't rob his own nest.

The person who plants thorns must
never expect to gather roses.

Proverbs 10:3

The LORD does not let the righteous go hungry, but he thwarts the craving of the wicked.

The Lord will not let the righteous go hungry, but He denies the wicked what they crave. **(HCSB)**

The LORD does not let good people go hungry, but he keeps evil people from getting what they want. **(NCV)**

Be blessed and let God handle the rest.

God won't let the righteous go hungry or his children beg for bread.

To whom God gives, to him also the people give.

Proverbs 10:5

A child who gathers in summer is prudent, but a child who sleeps in harvest brings shame.

He who gathers in summer is a son who acts wisely, But he who sleeps in harvest is a son who acts shamefully. **(NASB)**

Those who gather crops on time are wise, but those who sleep through the harvest are a disgrace. **(NCV)**

The teeth chew that the stomach will be filled.

The world is full of willing people: Some willing to work and some willing to let them.

Proverbs 10:7

*The memory of the righteous is a blessing,
but the name
of the wicked will rot.*

*Good people will be remembered as a
blessing, but evil people will soon be
forgotten.* **(NCV)**

*The memory of the upright is a blessing,
but the name of the evil-doer will be turned
to dust.* **(BBE)**

Only what you do for Christ will last.

Old sins cast long shadows.

Gratitude is the heart's memory.

Write kindness in marble and write injuries in the dust.

Proverbs 10:26

As vinegar to the teeth,
and as smoke to the eyes,
so is the sluggard to them that send him.

A lazy person affects the one he works for
like vinegar on the teeth
or smoke in the eyes. **(NCV)**

Like vinegar to the teeth and smoke to the
eyes, so the slacker is to the one who sends
him on an errand. **(HCSB)**

Lazy people get on your last nerve.

Empty sacks will never stand upright.

It's the empty can that makes the most noise.

Proverbs 3:27

Withhold not good from them to whom it is due, when it is in the power of thine hand to do it.

Whenever you are able, do good to people who need help. **(NCV)**

Do not withhold good from those to whom it is due, when it is in your power to do it. **(RSV)**

What goes around comes around.

Do to others what you would want them do to you.

Proverbs 5:15

Drink waters out of thine own cistern, and running waters out of thine own well.

Drink water out of your own cistern and running water from your own well. **(GWD)**

Drink the water from your own cistern, fresh water from your own well. **(CJB)**

You are the best person to define yourself.

The grass is not always greener on the other side.

Let your bucket down where you are.

It is the good horse that draws its own cart.

You don't have to take your rented car to the car wash.

Proverbs 6:6

Go to the ant, thou sluggard; consider her ways, and be wise

Go watch the ants, you lazy person. Watch what they do and be wise. **(NCV)**

Go to the ant, you lazybones! Consider its ways, and be wise. **(CJB)**

Who told the ant that it can lift more than its weight?

If the myth says it can't, why does the bumble bee fly?

Proverbs 10:18

*He that hideth hatred with lying lips, and
he that uttereth a slander, is a fool.*

*Whoever hides hate is a liar. Whoever tells
lies is a fool.* **(NCV)**

*The one who conceals hatred has lying
lips, and whoever
spreads slander is a fool.* **(HCSB)**

Don't hate people hate their ways.

A great talker is a great liar.

Proverbs 10:24

The fear of the wicked, it shall come upon him: but the desire of the righteous shall be granted.

Evil people will get what they fear most, but good people will get what they want most. **(NCV)**

What the wicked fear, will overtake them, But the desire of the righteous will be granted. **(HNV)**

You become who you think you are.

A good beginning makes a good ending.

If you have never done anything evil,
you should not be worrying about devils
knocking at your door.

If you do well for the devil, out of
gratitude he will deliver you to hell.

To thine own self be true.

Proverbs 11:1

A false balance is abomination to the LORD: but a just weight is his delight.

A false balance is an abomination to the LORD, but a just weight is his delight. **(RSV)**

Dishonest scales are disgusting to the LORD, but accurate weights are pleasing to him. **(WEB)**

God doesn't like ugly.

A squirrel is just a rat with good PR.

Proverbs 29:18

Where there is no vision, the people perish: but he that keepeth the law, happy is he.

Where there is no vision, the people are uncontrolled; but he who keeps the law will be happy. **(BBE)**

Where there is no revelation, the people cast off restraint; But one who keeps the law is blessed. **(HNV)**

If you don't where you are going you are apt to get lost.

Any fool can criticize, condemn and complain, and most do.

A good life lived today makes every yesterday a dream of a good future, and every morning a vision of hope.

Great minds think alike, simple minds can't think of anything different.

Proverbs 13:17

A wicked messenger falleth into mischief:
but a faithful ambassador is health.

A wicked messenger brings nothing but
trouble, but a trustworthy one makes
everything right. **(NCV)**

An undependable messenger gets into
trouble, but a dependable envoy brings
healing. **(GWD)**

Watch the messenger and don't always
blame the message.

The person who brings good news
knocks hard.

The person who seeks trouble never misses.

Proverbs 14:4

Where no oxen are, the crib is clean: but much increase is by the strength of the ox.

Where there are no cattle, the feeding trough is empty, but the strength of an ox produces plentiful harvests. **(GWD)**

When there are no oxen, no food is in the barn. But with a strong ox, much grain can be grown. **(NCV)**

It doesn't always take a lot of people to get a lot done.

If the wind will not serve, take to the oars.

I pointed out to you the stars and all you saw was the tip of my finger.

If life deals you lemons make lemonade.

The person who stays in the valley won't get over the hill.

Proverbs 14:14

The backslider in heart shall be filled with his own ways: and a good man shall be satisfied from himself.

Evil people will be paid back for their evil ways, and good people will be rewarded for their good ones. **(NCV)**

The unfaithful will be repaid for his own ways; Likewise a good man will be rewarded for his ways. **(HNV)**

You get what you pay for.

A good conscience is the best divinity.

A clear conscience is a soft pillow.

A guilty conscience needs no accuser.

Proverbs 16:14

The wrath of a king is as messengers of death: but a wise man will pacify it.

The wrath of the king is like those who give news of death, but a wise man will put peace in place of it. **(BBE)**

An angry king can put someone to death, so a wise person will try to make him happy. **(NCV)**

Don't bite the hands that feed you.

A still tongue keeps a wise head.

Unspoken words are the flowers of silence.

When you have spoken the word, it reigns over you. When it is unspoken you reign over it.

Unspoken words cannot be noted.

Quarrels end, but words once spoken never die.

The best word still has to be spoken.

The spoken word sometimes loses what silence has won.

Four things come not back: The spoken word, the spent arrow, the past life, and the neglected opportunity.

Proverbs 17:17

*A friend loveth at all times, and a
brother is born for adversity.*

*A friend is loving at all times,
and becomes a brother
in times of trouble.* **(BBE)**

*A friend loves you all the time, and a
brother helps in time of trouble.* **(NCV)**

**In the time of trouble is when you
know who your friends are.**

Blood is thicker than water.

Blue are the hills that are far away.

There is no need like the lack of a friend.

Proverbs 18:17

He that is first in his own cause seemeth just; but his neighbour cometh and searcheth him.

He who pleads his cause first seems right; Until another comes and questions him. **(HNV)**

The first to state his case seems right until another comes and cross-examines him. **(HCSB)**

Every story has at least two sides.

Prejudice is prejudging.

Proverbs 19:18

Chasten thy son while there is hope, and let not thy soul spare for his crying.

Correct your children while there is still hope; do not let them destroy themselves. **(NCV)**

Discipline your son while there is still hope. Do not be the one responsible for his death. **(GWD)**

Love your children with discipline.

Don't let your dreams become your nightmares.

Small children may give you headache
but it may be better than big children
giving you heartache.

Like parents like children.

Proverbs 20:14

It is naught, it is naught, saith the buyer:
but when he is gone his way,
then he boasteth.

Bad, bad," says the buyer, But when he
goes his way, then he boasts. **(NASB)**

"It's no good, it's no good," says the buyer;
But when he is gone his way, then he
boasts. **(HNV)**

Words don't always say what they mean.

One beats the bush, another takes the bird.

One person's loss is another person's gain.

Proverbs 20:17

Bread of deceit is sweet to a man; but afterwards his mouth shall be filled with gravel.

Food gained dishonestly tastes sweet to a person, but afterwards his mouth will be filled with gravel. **(GWD)**

Food gained by fraud is sweet to a man, but afterwards his mouth is full of gravel. **(HCSB)**

Your bad deeds will find you.

Quickly come, quickly go.

Dishonest money dwindles away. The person who gathers money little by little makes it grow.

Proverbs 20:24

Man's goings are of the Lord; how can a man then understand his own way?

The LORD is the one who directs a person's steps. How then can anyone understand his own way? **(GWD)**

The LORD decides what a person will do; no one understands what his life is all about. **(NCV)**

God knew you before you were born.

It is God who orders a person's steps.

Proverbs 25:12

As an earring of gold, and an ornament of fine gold, so is a wise reprover upon an obedient ear.

A wise warning to someone who will listen is as valuable as gold earrings or fine gold jewelry. **(NCV)**

Like a gold ring and a fine gold ornament, so is constructive criticism to the ear of one who listens. **(GWD)**

Active listening is better than hearing: "I told you so."

The moon does not listen to a barking dog.

A wise person hears one word and understands two.

Dr. Beresford Adams is a graduate of Princeton
Theological Seminary and Drew University